CONTENTS

KU-714-050

BRIGHT LIGHT

We need light to see and to stay alive.

LIGHT AND DARK

We see using light. Without light, it is **dark**. The darker it is, the harder it is to see. When it is completely dark, we cannot see anything at all.

It's dark in here! Now where are those cookies...?

Yum

LIFE-GIVER

Light is very important. As well as letting us see, light from the Sun helps plants to grow. If there were no plants to eat, there would be no animals or people on Earth.

RAYS OF LIGHT

Light travels in straight lines, called **rays**. You can sometimes see rays of light when the Sun is behind clouds, or shining through trees.

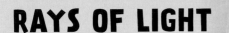

Can't catch me!

WOW!

Light is the fastest thing in the universe. If you could travel at the same speed as light, you could go round the Earth 7.5 times in a single second!

LIGHT SOURCES

Light is given off by natural and man-made sources.

MAKING LIGHT

Something that gives off light is called a **light source**. The Sun is our main light source. Light sources can be natural or man-made.

I can't give off light.

Here, just reflect mine instead!

NATURAL SOURCES

The Sun is a natural light source, and so is lightning. The Moon is not a light source, because it doesn't make its own light. Instead, it **reflects** light from the Sun.

Thanks guys!

WOW! --------

Some types of mushroom glow in the dark! The ability of some living things to give off is called **bioluminescence**.

MAN-MADE SOURCES

Some light sources are made by people. These include electric lights such as torches, and the lights in our houses. Candles and fireworks are other man-made light sources.

HEY, WHAT AM I?

Not all man-made light sources are used to light things up. What is the light source in this picture? Answer on page 28.

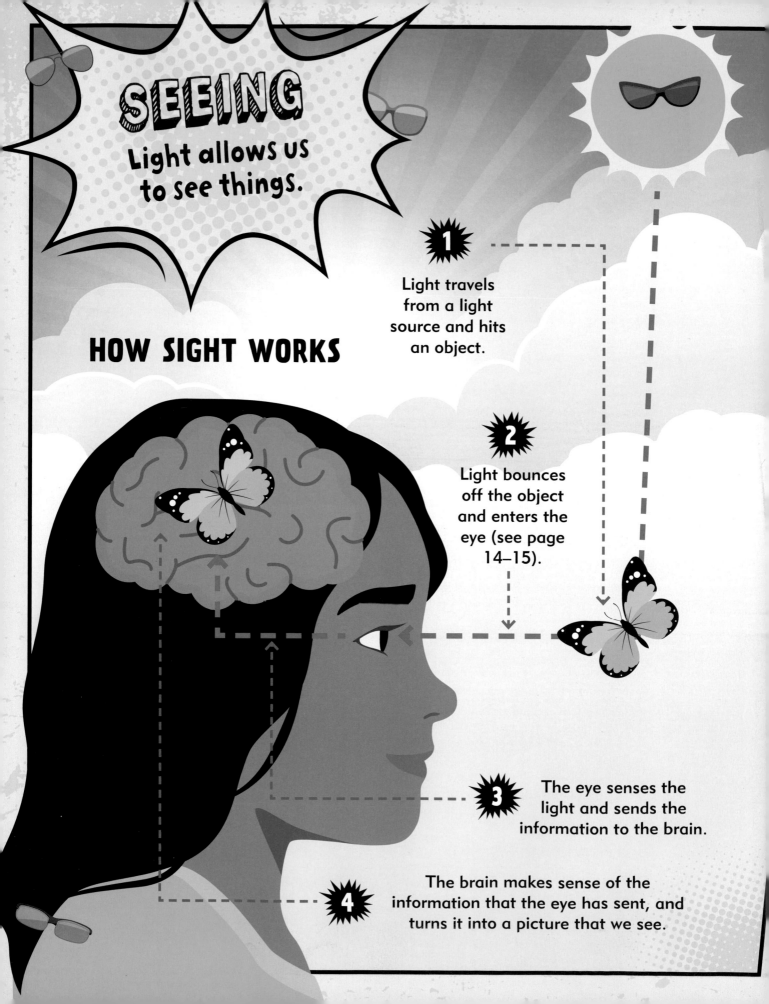

It's cool to protect your eyes.

STAYING SAFE

We need light to see, but light from the Sun is very strong. Wearing sunglasses on sunny days helps protect your eyes, but even with sunglasses on, you should never look directly at the Sun.

HIDE AND SEEK

How many pairs of sunglasses can you spot? Answer on page 28.

The giant squid has the biggest eyes in the world. At 28 cm across, they are as big as dinner plates!

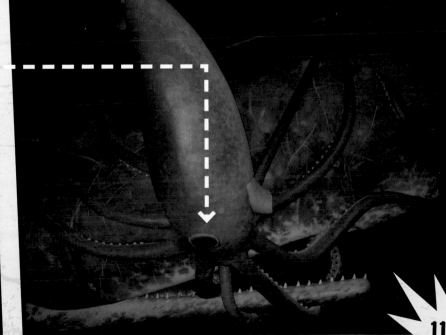

YOUR TURN!

EYES VS. BRAIN

What you see is a picture made by your brain, using information sent from your eyes. Trick your brain with this experiment. You'll need:

A sheet of A4 paper

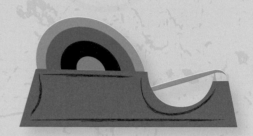

A roll of sticky tape

STEP ONE

Roll the piece of paper into a tube, lengthways. Stop it from unrolling with some pieces of sticky tape.

Hold the tube up to your right eye and look through it, keeping both eyes open. You should see what is going on around the tube, as well as the inside of the tube.

STEP THREE

Hold your left hand open with a flat palm, and place the side of it up against the tube, about two-thirds of the way down. Keep both eyes open. Experiment with moving your flat palm nearer and further from your eye. Now what can you see? Why do you think that is? Answer on page 28.

Ooooh!

13

REFLECTING LIGHT

When light hits surfaces, it bounces off them again.

BOING!

BOING!

REFLECTING

It can be funny to think of light bouncing, as though it were a rubber ball! But just like a ball, when light hits a surface, it bounces off and starts travelling in another direction. This is called reflecting.

SHINY THINGS

Some objects or surfaces reflect more light than others. Shiny surfaces such as metal or glass reflect a lot more light than **dull** surfaces such as wood or rock.

MIRRORS

When light bounces off a very flat, shiny surface such as a mirror or still water, it creates a **reflection**. This is a picture of whatever the light bounced off before it hit the mirror's surface.

What has the hairdresser done?!

HIDE AND SEEK

Something in the night sky reflects light. Can you spot it hiding? Answer on page 28.

HEY, WHAT AM I?

Reflective surfaces can be very useful. What can you see in this picture? Answer on page 28.

LIGHT AND MATERIALS

Light passes through some materials, but not others.

TRANSPARENT

Materials such as glass or clear plastic let light through them. Because light passes through them, you can see through them too. These materials are called **transparent**.

Eek! A cat! I'm glad this table is opaque.

OPAQUE

Many of the materials that we use every day, such as wood, metal and coloured plastic, do not let light through. These are **opaque** materials.

TRANSLUCENT

Some materials let a bit of light through, but partly block the rays. These materials are **translucent**. You can't see clearly through them, but you can see light, and outlines.

HEY, WHAT AM I?

Which of these objects on the shelf are transparent, translucent and opaque? Answer on page 29.

Don't forget to turn off the windows!

WOW!

Scientists have invented a special type of coating for glass windows. Called 'electrochromic glass', it turns your windows from transparent to opaque at the flick of a switch!

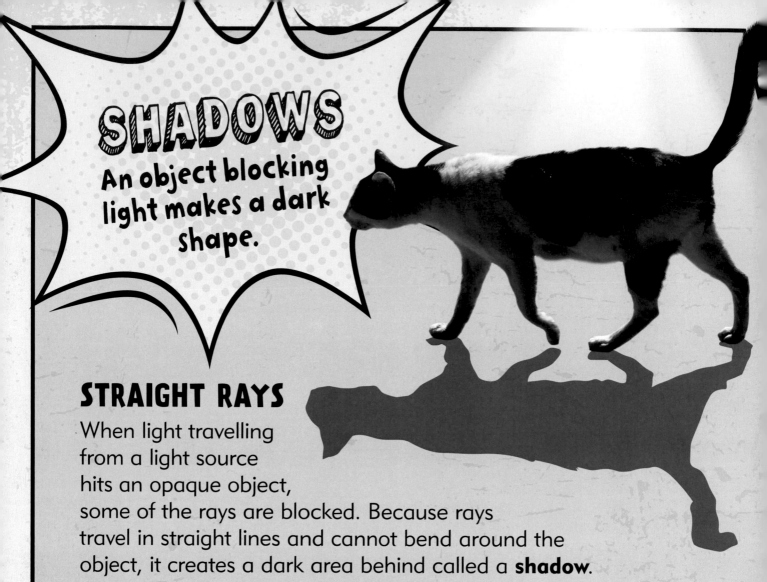

SHADOWS
An object blocking light makes a dark shape.

STRAIGHT RAYS

When light travelling from a light source hits an opaque object, some of the rays are blocked. Because rays travel in straight lines and cannot bend around the object, it creates a dark area behind called a **shadow**.

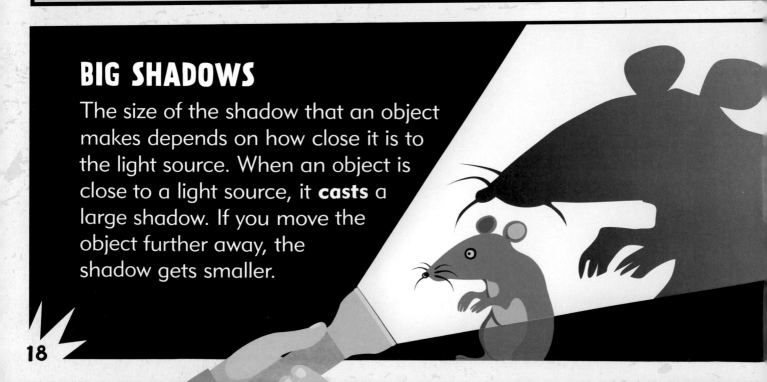

BIG SHADOWS

The size of the shadow that an object makes depends on how close it is to the light source. When an object is close to a light source, it **casts** a large shadow. If you move the object further away, the shadow gets smaller.

SHADOW ANGLE

Have you noticed how your shadow changes length and position throughout the day? This is because the Sun is moving through the sky. This means light comes from different directions at different times of day.

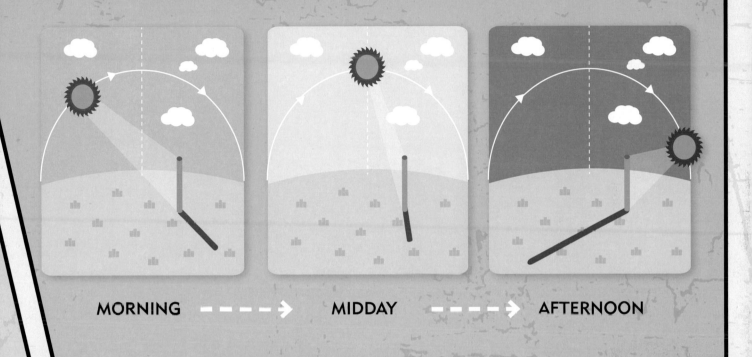

MORNING ------> MIDDAY ------> AFTERNOON

HEY, WHAT AM I?

In the past, people used to tell the time using the changing position of the Sun in the sky. Do you know what this object is called?
Answer on page 29.

SILHOUETTE PORTRAITS

Explore how shadows get larger and smaller depending on the distance from a light source with this activity. You'll need:

A pencil

Scissors

A bright torch or lamp

A friend

A chair

Sticky tack

Several A3 sheets of coloured paper

STEP ONE

Find an area of wall where you can stick up a piece of A3 paper using sticky tack, with space to sit in front of it. Have your friend sit on the chair right next to the paper on the wall, facing sideways.

Position the lamp so that it is close to your friend's face, casting a large shadow of their head on the paper behind. Trace around the edge of the shadow with the pencil while your friend sits very still.

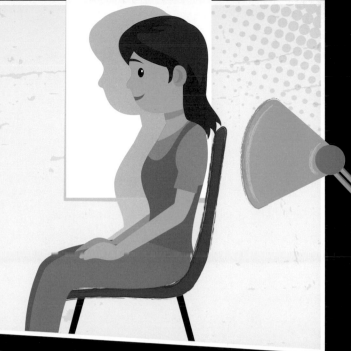

STEP THREE

Put up a new piece of paper. This time, move the lamp further away to make a differently-sized **silhouette** of your friend's head. Then, swap over and have them trace around your shadow.

STEP FOUR

Cut your silhouette portraits out! If you like you can glue them onto a piece of different coloured paper to create a piece of art.

Did you know that humans need some light from the Sun to stay healthy? Our bodies use sunlight to get an important **nutrient** called vitamin D from our food. It helps keep our bones strong.

COLD ZONE

Places such as **Antarctica** are very cold and dry, and in winter there is no sunlight at all. To survive without sun, emperor penguins in Antarctica have to go the whole winter without eating, huddled together to keep warm.

HIDE AND SEEK

Although a bit of sunlight is healthy, too much sun can burn your skin. What things can you use to stay safe in the sun? Can you spot them hiding?

Answer on page 29.

LIGHTS AT NIGHT

Man-made sources of light are very important in our day-to-day lives. One of the most obvious uses of man-made light is to see what we are doing at night-time.

MAKING ELECTRICITY

Light from the Sun is very powerful. It is so powerful that we can capture it using **solar panels** to make **electricity**, which helps power some of our homes and cities.

SENDING MESSAGES

Throughout history, people have used lights to tell each other things or give instructions. Flashing lights can be used to say things using **Morse code**. Every day, traffic lights tell people when to stop and when to go.

BEING SEEN

Light can help us see... and be seen! When it's dark, glowing lights can show us where things are. The red rear light on the back of a bicycle lets drivers know where the cyclist is.

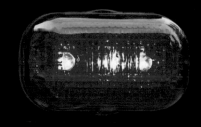

HEY, WHAT AM I?

This glowing light is showing you where something is. What is it? Answer on page 29.

CHAT USING LIGHT

Use light to send messages in Morse Code. You'll need:

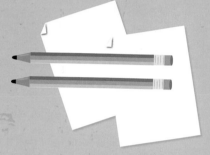

Pencils and some paper

Two copies of the Morse code

Two torches (the more powerful the better)

A friend   **An adult**

STEP ONE

Get ready...

Ask your adult to take you and a friend to a big open space, such as a playing field, in the evening when it is dark. Each take a torch, and a pencil and some paper, and stand at either end of the playing field.

Don't go anywhere at night without an adult!

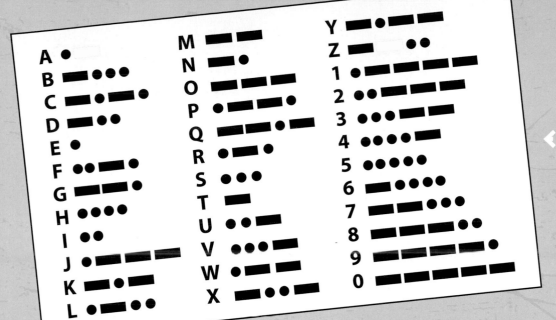

The Morse code

STEP TWO

Using this Morse code alphabet, spell out messages to one another by flashing your torch on and off. Flash it quickly for a dot, and give a longer flash for a dash. Leave a gap between letters and a long gap between words. As your friend flashes a message, note down the dots and dashes on your paper so you can translate the coded message.

Why can using light sometimes be better for sending messages than sound? Answer on page 29.

OK, that was dot, dash, dot ...

FLASH! FLASH!

27

ANSWERS

Page 9

What am I? I'm a television.

Page 11 **Hide and Seek** Sunglasses

SEEING
Sight allows us to see things.

HOW SIGHT WORKS

1 Light travels from a light source and hits the object.

2 Light bounces off the object and enters the eye.

3 The eye senses the light and sends the information to the brain.

4 The brain makes sense of the information that the eye has sent, and turns it into a picture that we see.

It's cool to protect your eyes.

STAYING SAFE
We need light to see, but light from the Sun is very strong. Wearing sunglasses on sunny days helps protect your eyes, but even with sunglasses you should never look directly at the Sun.

HIDE AND SEEK
How many pairs of sunglasses can you spot? Answer on page 28.

WOW!
The giant squid has the biggest eyes in the world. At 28 cm across, they are as big as dinner plates!

Page 13

Your turn
When you hold your hand up to the side of the tube, you can see a 'hole' in your hand. This is because both your eyes are sending the light information to your brain at the same time. Your brain is trying to make sense of the two sets of information, to make a single 'picture' of what you see. The best it can do is show a hole in your hand!

Page 15

REFLECTING LIGHT
When light hits surfaces, it bounces off again.

BOING!

BOING!

REFLECTION
It can be funny to think of light bouncing, as though it is a rubber ball! But just like a ball, when light hits a surface, it bounces off and starts travelling in another direction. This is called reflecting.

SHINY THINGS
Some objects or surfaces reflect more light than others. Shiny surfaces such as metal or glass reflect a lot more light than **dull** surfaces such as wood or rock.

MIRRORS
When light bounces off a very flat, shiny surface such as a mirror or still water, it creates a **reflection**. This is a picture of whatever the light bounced off before it hit the mirror's surface.

What has the hairdresser done!

HIDE AND SEEK
Something in the night sky reflects light. Can you spot it hiding? Answer on page 28.

HEY, WHAT AM I?
Reflective surfaces can be very useful. What can you see in this picture? Answer on page 28.

Hide and Seek The Moon

Page 15

What am I? I'm a person wearing dark clothing and a reflective jacket.

Page 17

What am I?

1 I'm a transparent glass jar.

2 I'm an opaque wooden giraffe.

3 I'm a translucent coloured glass vase.

Page 19

What am I? I'm a sundial.

Page 23

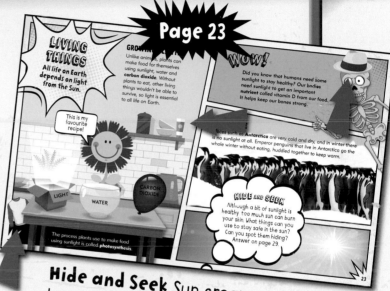

Hide and Seek Sun cream, sun hat, long-sleeved shirt

Page 25

What am I? I'm an emergency exit sign.

Page 27

Your turn

One reason that light is sometimes better for sending messages is that bright light can travel much further than sound, while staying clear. Light is often used for sending messages at sea for this reason.

GLOSSARY

Antarctica the continent located at the southern end of the Earth

bioluminescence light given off by living things such as plants and insects

carbon dioxide one of the gases that is in the air we breathe

cast to cause a shadow or an area of light on a surface

dark when there is no light, it is dark

dull not shiny or reflective

electricity energy that we use to make things such as lamps and TVs work

light source something that gives off light

Morse code a code where letters and numbers are translated into dots and dashes

nutrient goodness found in food

opaque doesn't let light through, so you can't see through it

photosynthesis the way plants make food for themselves using light

rays straight lines of light that spread out from one point

reflect when light hits a surface and bounces off

reflection a picture that is created on a surface when light bounces off it

shadow a dark area made when light is blocked by an object

silhouette a dark shape made by something that has light behind it

solar panels objects that take light from the Sun and turn it into electricity

translucent lets some light through so you can see shapes, but not details

transparent lets enough light through so that you can clearly see through it

INDEX